MY LIFE AS A GODARD MOVIE

*15 faits divers sur ma
vie comme un film de
Jean-Luc Godard*

Joanna Walsh

**TRANSIT
BOOKS**

Published by Transit Books
2301 Telegraph Avenue, Oakland, California 94612
www.transitbooks.org

© 2021 Joanna Walsh
ISBN: 978-1-945492-64-8 (paperback) | 978-1-945492-68-6 (ebook)
LIBRARY OF CONGRESS CONTROL NUMBER: 2022939667

COVER DESIGN
Anna Morrison

TYPESETTING
Justin Carder

DISTRIBUTED BY
Consortium Book Sales & Distribution
(800) 283-3572 | cbsd.com

Printed in the United States of America

9 8 7 6 5 4 3 2 1

This project is supported in part by an award from the National
Endowment for the Arts.

MY LIFE AS A
GODARD MOVIE

Within the framework of conventional understanding, the desire for a New Look skirt cannot be seen as a political want, let alone a proper one.
—Carolyn Steedman, *Landscape for a Good Woman*

LA CHINOISE—RED

If, approaching the end of the world, we're forced to choose a single surviving monument to human art, it won't be how any particular work looks, but the act of looking. We know that already, but how can looking be recorded? I guess in paint or stone, but it's better in photographs and best in film. I like film because the paint is human. So many paintings have been made about women by men, the women's gaze only pigment the man has put there: on camera the woman is a real person and, no matter how much the director tries to turn her into a colour, there she is looking through the mask of the colours that make up the makeup on her face, and also her face, her hair, her eyes.

Before I taught myself to paint, I never used the colour green. I'd go as far as the sour, dark turquoise of tables and other objects in my childhood's schools. I wanted to live in primary colour; something uncompromised that couldn't be mixed from anything else. A man once looked at me and said I looked like I was filmed in Eastmancolor. That was the colour filmstock Jean-Luc Godard used, and Godard didn't like green either. His films take place against the pale limestone city of Paris or the pale sand-coloured earth of the Maquis. Add the blue of the Mediterranean—and sometimes his characters wear red. There are no secondary colours in Godard and green is a secondary colour.

I've been thinking about Godard because of the insideness of his film *La Chinoise*, in which a cell of teen Maoists hide out in an Hausmannian apartment where they helplessly play out the gender, race and class structures they've quarantined themselves against. The film takes place in interiors, where the colours are entirely controlled both by the camera and available resources. Godard liked to show this—some of the walls are works in progress—and I have some degree of nostalgia for having a man tell me what colour I am, and this is partly a nostalgia for my own willingness to subject myself to entire aesthetic control by another, as a work in progress, and specifically by a man, out of curiosity, to find out something about men and what they desire. And that nostalgia has a colour.

There have been essays about falling in love with a colour; how about falling in hate?

When I began to teach myself to paint, I became obsessed with capturing green. What colour shifts more, what shade can be mixed from a wider palette of other colours and still hook to its name? I endlessly copied the mid-twentieth century British artist Edward Ardizzone's green-layered-over-dirt-red watercolour wash. What looked more like ground? Not the squares of violent turf I'd grown up with, designed to keep the weeds down between marmalade-bricked blocks. They looked like astroturf—and wouldn't that have been more convenient for upkeep and consistency? That colour—the WhatsApp logo; the FaceTime logo—is cold sports halls and terrifying walks home between municipal playing fields. It is terror. The green we're told is green is not a colour. It resembles nothing in nature, though we're told it does and that, when we get our first box of paints, this is the colour we should paint the earth, and the colour we should love as though it were the earth—the same kind of lie that told me I should enjoy living within those secondary-colour bricked angles—accommodation that, real enough, refused to accommodate anything but its own reality—and that I should not think of changing my spots. In a little while I would be able to push a pram there around the square of green-approximating nature. That green could not be worn down or changed. I prefer art to life. But it has to be the right art.

Louise Bourgeois hated green too. 'If someone wore a green shirt she would ask him to change it,' wrote her assistant, Jerry Gorovoy, soon after her death, 'or she would refuse to look at him.'[1] He doesn't say why.

Though it was not a deliberate choice, at least three of the men who have looked at me have had green eyes, and two of them have looked at me with this green gaze across a number of years. Green is a recessive eye colour, which means increasingly few people see through its lens. But if you looked into the irises of those three men closely, you would see that they were made up, not of a solid colour, but of small strands, some of which were not green at all.

There's a resistance, in Godard's women, that is at the heart of his work (and theirs). And it's in the way they look at Godard's men. Their uncomprehending faces, turned to his camera (or his protagonist) are, I guess, the 'eternal irony of the community'.[2] They are something the camera finds alien, filmed finding something alien. They desire the man, but they don't know what the man is, and they're quite aware that, though he may satisfy some of their needs, he may be otherwise incomprehensible, difficult, dangerous. They look out of curiosity, to find out something about men. They look and they evaluate, not only the men, but their chances.

Godard, who is said to have advertised for a 'lead actress and girlfriend' (and found Anna Karina), isn't often thought of—in his early films at least—as a feminist film maker[3], but that moment of resistance he notices in his women, his study of their hesitation, of the kind of interest that holds its object at a distance, is something I do not often see recognised.

And it's not true that Godard never uses green: he uses sage, he uses sea-green; he uses eau-de-nil, he sometimes uses green that is almost black. At other times, fields and trees intrude: how would they not? Of Godard's regular stars, Jean-Paul Belmondo's eyes are said by some websites to be 'green-grey', and others, 'dark brown'; Anna Karina's: 'blue', Anne Wiazemsky's: 'no info'; Jean-Pierre Léaud's: 'N/A'. I don't know Godard's eye colour. Perhaps it is the colour of the camera lens.

Green has looked at me. At the end of the world, the monument to human art will not be any art object but a kind of look. It will have green eyes, and it will look at nothing green.

Imagine a world of only three colours: red, yellow and blue.

PART 1:

BLACK

AND

WHITE

LE PETIT SOLDAT—GREY

I don't watch films in the dark, in the cinema, or even on a screen as big as a television. I watch *Le petit soldat* in daylight on my laptop in my kitchen with the dishwasher on. Even fullscreen gives me claustrophobia. I watch films with a border of life round the edge, my life.

Or perhaps what I need is escape.

Before the green gaze, there was black and white. So many of Godard's '60s black and white films take place in Paris, but not this one. The Godard films I watch are New Wave, released before 1968. I was conceived in 1969 and born in 1970, bridging the cusp of the decade. My parents married two years before my birth: yes, in the summer of '68 they made the *'least radical gesture'*[4] (which, to be fair, years later, I also made) and prepared to live in a world of secondary colours—teal, orange and brown—which we called the '70s.

For what were cars designed? For parents and children. There's no family in Godard. Only in *Pierrot le fou*, where it's quickly blown apart. What looks odd in a car? Four grown men, two in kid seats in the back. Here they are, and here, alone, is Anna Karina (Godard's women are lone or, sometimes, move in pairs but never in groups). In the car, Karina looks in the mirror as she does in *Bande à part*, combs her hair like Chantal Goya in *Masculin féminin*. What is she checking? That she is beautiful? That she's still there?

> Godard plots are driven by desire.
> For excitement, money, utopia, sex but seldom love.
> Love is their by-product; beauty its currency.
> (Karina is at first the subject of an exchange of money between men.)

Two men desire Anna Karina. We don't know if she desires either, or anyone else. She does not act as though she has desire. Some men don't ever think about desire in a woman. Or there's something about it they don't want to think about. They prefer her to be desired without showing signs of desiring.

(Or is Godard depicting this situation?)

What's a green gaze? To be green-eyed is to envy, or to desire. These are two different things: to desire is to want; to envy is to want to be. Green is a quality not of the envied but the envier. A green gaze is *in* the eye of the beholder, so seldom shown beholding. The green gaze holds its subject: it is everything its subject is not.

In Godard, beauty and violence are linked—but he's set this up already. 'Ethics are the aesthetics of the future,' I transcribe obediently, as Godard's protagonist, Bruno, dismisses all women over twenty-five. Godard first married a twenty-, then nineteen-year-old, as though he could rewind to match each. What is it about youth he couldn't shake? When Bruno says it's unfair that women age it's unclear if he means for him or for them.

Then Godard kills Karina again. Or rather, for the first time, as he will in *Vivre sa vie*, *Pierrot le fou*, though this time we don't see. He shoots. With a gun, with a camera. She is shot. Godard can kill her. Can give her life again.

Can replay this many times. 'The privilege of the dead,' says Bruno, 'is not to die again.' When Karina dies it's at a double distance because the subs unsynch. I hear the words but don't quite trust my French. I think I know what's happening, but I'm not sure.

> *(Why did I make the 'least radical gesture' that brought me back to the green square I'd worked so hard to leave? Because I'd wanted a revolution that was 'fair': a revolution without violence; a revolution without beauty. I knew it was unfair that only beautiful girls got the chance to appear, and unfair that violence destroyed them. I wanted to have a revolution by revolutionising appearance.)*

Still there is no arguing with the movement of Karina's head turning toward, or away from, the camera, her every normal gesture—photographable!

Beauty is not an experience for the beautiful, but the eye, the mirror, the lens. Cinema, Bruno claims, is 'truth at 24 frames per second'.[5] If beauty is truth and truth, beauty, does something unbeautiful happen between the frames, or are they gaps of beauty we never see?

What do I desire from this beauty? And what does it want from me?

If I watch beauty for long enough can I find any *point commun?*

And the dishwasher says, *aucun, aucun, aucun*…[6]

À BOUT DE SOUFFLE—WHITE

Desire to see beauty replayed is very much like the desire for beautiful clothes.

In what ways has learning how to dress taught me how to live?

When I see Belmondo move on-screen I'm reminded how men's worlds and clothes are designed to fit their bodies, whilst women's bodies have to fit their clothes and the worlds they find themselves in.

'Why buy a dress from Dior when there are great dresses in Tati?' Belmondo asks Seberg.

Which reminds me of the man who asked me,

—*'Why spend money on a dress when you could buy a ticket to Paris?'*

— *'But what would I wear when I got there?'*

As it turns out, everything that happens in the next scene hinges on the dress. Seberg is noticed because of it, and what is noticed is that she's beautiful. There is a 'role' in the world, a famous author tells her, for beautiful women wearing beautiful dresses. But only for them.

(How many things have I left undone because I was not 'beautiful' enough?
How many things have I dared because I was dressed for it?)

Whatever. It's a pleasure to read Seberg's appearance: her beauty a contrast to the stiff chic of her clothes.

The green gaze of envy is solved by identification: if I can't be as beautiful as Seberg, perhaps I can dress like her. The women I know who can afford beautiful clothes are rich, and even they can't afford Dior. For everyone else, aspiring to chic will do. It has to. In Paris, chic does not mean 'ineffable'. It means 'smart'. In Paris it is possible, even easy, to be 'too' chic: perfection is *imparfaite*, which in no way means 'unbeautiful'. Is it possible to desire a revolution without this desire that's like the compromised desire for beautiful clothes, now perfect imperfection has become more bourgeois than aspiring to bourgeois-chic?

I have studied Godard's movies by trying to live them, and I have tried to live them by dressing for them. I didn't want a Dior dress but, aged seventeen (like Anne in *Vladimir et Rosa*) I worked painstakingly to make a t-shirt that said 'NEW YORK HERALD TRIBUNE', a hand-painted imitation of a corporate logo. Pre-internet I copied it from the frozen blur of a video frame.

I wanted it that much.

I did not paint it perfectly, but I did it with such determination, attention to detail and reasonable skill, that it seemed, for a while, an adequate substitute.

I always wanted, not the real, but to make by hand an idea, and that my handiwork should have the polish of capital.

(To try to live by fiction is a risky pursuit, especially when the video quality is not good.)

How do you stare at someone until they stop staring at you? (À bout de souffle). *Seberg eyes Belmondo through a lens made from a rolled up paper; as Karina does through a record's turntable hole in* Le petit soldat: *the director's feminine avatars.*

The camera never blinks first.

MASCULIN FÉMININ—BLACK

It's only when you've seen several Godard movies that you begin to understand what a Godard movie is.

I feel trepidation beginning to watch this film, but I'm too tired to work in any other way.

Fun… fun… I do not watch films for fun.

How is it to be a Parisien(ne) watching Godard's Paris, locked down in a reality of his imagination? Or do Parisien(ne)s take it for granted that they live in a movie?

What do I miss when I miss Paris so much? What do they?

I greenscreen my Zoom background and drop in the interior of Godard's apartment, where he filmed *La Chinoise*: white walls, blue door, blue-grey carpet, red chairs. The wall behind me now says: 'IL FAUT CONFRONTER LES IDÉES VAGUES AVEC DES IMAGES CLAIRES.'[7]

(All this before I even begin to watch. All this to prepare myself.)

i

Like the apartment in *La Chinoise*, Godard films are an enclosed world. Nevertheless they attempt border crossings: in *La Chinoise,* the borders of an apartment; in *Le Mépris*, in *Pierrot le fou*, the borders of a country; in *Masculin féminin* (and *Bande à part*), the borders of the city. *Masculin féminin* doesn't take place in *Paris* Paris but a Paris that's being destroyed and a Paris that's being built. Knowing there was no revolutionary potential in a beautiful city, why did Godard cling to revolutionary potential in beautiful girls?

(I have wanted to write this book for a long time.
Perhaps I can write it only now that Paris is no longer an option.)

Masculin féminin's 'Zoo Café' just inside the Eastern Périphérique, the ring road that separates Paris from *Paris* Paris, is possibly now C'sters (3.9 on Google Reviews: 'Ten tables per server is inhuman'). And I wish I were Chantal Goya, not because she was beautiful but because, replaying the film, she is still sitting in the café where they serve 'confusingly banal' pancakes; because I can revisit her thereness in Paris as—not having filmed my life—I cannot revisit my own.

I think about Paris all the time. The last time I thought like this was the other time I was trapped by my life.
When I'm not in Godard, I feel displaced.

Near the possible café is a 'Villa Jean Godard' (an impasse; a dead-end street), missing the Luc(k).

Before, I wanted to go to Paris because it was impossible for me. Now that Paris is impossible for anyone outside Paris, I will act as though Godard's Paris is completely possible.

ii

Green screens are the least natural green: the green of crayons and astroturf, of an idea of nature that signals the difference between image and words. Acting against green screen means the actors can be isolated and their context replaced. It's easy to chromakey bright green: it's an inhuman colour few people wear. It's nobody's skin tone, and few people's eyes.

The last time I watched *Masculin féminin*, I might have been the same age as Chantal Goya's character, Madeleine: twenty-one. I remember the beauty but not the politics. Also I remember Goya's beauty but not Jean-Pierre Léaud's. I could not see Léaud for what he also was: a doll.

Léaud (unusually) presents as a man willing to be consumed.

(Belmondo presents as a man reluctant to be consumed.)

What happens when beauty becomes consumable?

Madeleine, a proto *yé-yé* popstar, shut in a recording booth alone, can hear her music through her headphones. All we hear is her voice responding. Madeleine sings, as the producer asks, 'very sweetly' about love. She does not sing about any specific lover, just the feeling of desire, and yes she sings 'very sweetly', but without any desire at all. She sings not to persuade anyone to love her but to persuade listeners to buy the shell of desire her song provides, in which to lodge theirs. 'I can't hear my voice,' Madeleine complains, 'there's too much echo.' Her boyfriend, Paul (Léaud), enters her glass box uninvited. She ignores him. He returns to where only the producer can hear the whole song. Madeleine cannot hear her voice. Only Paul heard Madeleine sing both with accompaniment and alone, only Paul and us.

When asked what is the centre of the world, Paul says, 'love', Madeleine says, 'me'.

I like to see Madeleine ignore Paul. I like to see that her work is more important than her work's subject; that she will not, IRL, do anything for love. When I first saw the film this seemed evidence of her coldness. Now it is evidence of her devotion, but not her devotion to a man. When I first saw the film I was devoted to a man, now I am devoted to my work. I can be devoted to people too but, as Madeleine knows, one cannot replace the other.

Madeline, asked what she desires, says, 'j'hésite'.

Real-life pop icon Françoise Hardy is seen briefly in the film, escorted from a US Embassy car into an official building wearing a ridiculous dress whose buttons and belt do not at all do their job but are mere ornament. Madeleine wears something similar, under a coat with a pocket embroidered with the letter C, and a matching striped scarf bearing the letter G: not her character's initials—Madeleine Klimmer—but CG: Chantal Goya.

Mr Director: can a woman's beauty be privatised? Once shot, you can sell it, lend it, rent it. The more she shows her beauty, the more its value increases: value that she or you can vend. But, being that value, she becomes less contained, detaches from her background. You can no longer hold on to the beauty you have made together, which would not exist without the camera.

Green screen is not made in the camera but post-production. It is not 'truth at 24 frames per second', but separates figures from their context. Godard did not use special effects, he wanted to show his characters in 'real' environments, yet they always remain separate, as though greenscreened, seemingly without roots or family commitments. Their jobs are transitory. Their politics are passionate, but not grassroots: the rights they demonstrate for are not their own. Though they are young, they are not naive: there is nothing green about them.

iii

Masculin féminin promises '*15 faits précis*' (*fait* = fact). Or '*15 precise acts*' (*fait* = deed). Two Godardian facets: truth and action. Perhaps they combine in *faits divers:* personal scandals in the local news, confined by intuited borders: a green square. I have been a local scandal, so local to myself I've not told it till now.

(ONE FAIT DIVERS I KNOW ABOUT ME:

Did I ever tell you I'm still alive because I went to Paris? Went to Paris, never having been there, but having a Paris to go to? Unhappily married (two words to stand in for so much), unable to decide to leave my green square, I thought (two words to stand in for so much) of death. Instead of dying, I went to Paris. The Eurostar was new, my ticket, a supermarket offer. I got up at 4 am, told no one; messaged to say I'd left early for work, would stay late. From the Gare du Nord I took the metro to Saint-Michel. Above ground I walked—tracing Paris's borders—west, then north, crossed the river, found the hill, walked without stopping for eight hours til I came back to Paris Nord where I took the train back to London. I did not even live in London, but three hours out: ten hours travel and eight hours walking: eighteen hours: a day, a day that saved my life.

I went to Paris because of Godard, amongst others.

I went to Paris because Godard showed me beauty I could recognise within conventional beauty's borders, but that beauty did not lead to that green square amongst square orange buildings. He showed me beauty as the power to say no or even, j'hésite. He showed me beauty decontextualised, greenscreened: beauty without romance.

'A relative liberty,' says Jean-Pierre Léaud in the opening scene.

I could not relive my youth and make another choice.

THIS IS A HYMN TO JEAN-LUC(K) GODARD'S PARIS, WHICH SAVED MY LIFE.
AND ALSO WHICH CONDEMNED ME.)

DOLLY STORY—TARMAC

Instead of watching *Une femme est une femme,* I watch *Dolly Story.*

Filmed in 1966, *Dolly Story* is a London documentary *not* made by Jean-Luc Godard. In the opening shots, the camera picks up girls on the street. They're dressed to impress, but anxious about who might see. At the crossings they *hésite* looking in every direction including behind before they cross. It's OK to make a decision, but you have to know the past and the future too: impossible! Which of my mother's generation of girls could have predicted me watching them now? Over the credits plays The Troggs' *With A Girl Like You*. Not seeing 'you', the camera restlessly searches for anyone 'like you'.

What is it to catch a glimpse of *a girl like you* when you do not desire a girl *like* her but desire to *be* like her? What kind of green gaze is that?

> *It was about this time I started an anonymous Instagram account to follow women in the street. I followed nobody I knew. I followed influencers, Parisiennes, often famous as girls in the '60s, or their children. For a while I followed these sons and daughters of the failed revolution as they walked the Paris streets, went to restaurants or their beach houses—this summer, all in France.*

> *(Tell me who you follow and I'll tell you who you are.)*[8]

> *Instagram, Tumblr, Pinterest: I can feed my eyes with beauty without cease. I come across an uncharacteristic photo of Françoise Hardy—who usually looks straight at the camera, serious: a musician—young, in a baby-doll dress and bloomers, suggestively sucking a lollipop; same hard stare. Despite her image (or as part of its complexity), Hardy sang 'very sweetly' like Goya in* Masculin féminin. *Hardy could look serious in any clothes because she had the sort of body that allowed her to ignore her body, without the uneven lines that can embarrass any outfit. Beauty as negative; you can't ignore Hardy's body. And that's why she can.*

Colour or black-and-white, the standard for film colour is measured by beautiful girls. 'China Girls'[9] are almost always white—in France they are all called 'Lili'— and young, their porcelain skin used in film production to calibrate 'natural' skin tone. This 'nature' is no less a cultural standard than their 'beauty'. Often wearing visible makeup, and occasionally replaced by real (plastic) dolls, the process of calibrating by their pale skin can cause darker faces to be underexposed.[10]

Shot once, China Girls remain in the studio for years after their originals have aged, or even died. Though tech has moved beyond the need to use this white girl standard, China Girls are still used as controls. Sold or given away by film labs, duplicated in batches, blown up… the white girl standard: a violence both to those it excludes and the girls who never asked to stand for this violence done to others.

Dolly Story shows Playboy bunnies and Mary Quant catwalkers: models of femininity with utterly opposed ideal bodies. The curvy bunnies smile; the angular models look stern, but they both end up stripped. One kind of nakedness is called 'traditional', the other 'radical'.

Their headshots often imply China Girls are naked beyond the frame. However much they're showing, they never appear in the films that use them. Each China Girl shot is less than a second of film. If cinema is 'truth at 24 frames per second,' and if *beauty is truth, truth beauty,* they are what falls between the frames.

Now, as then, girls are dressing for their lives. I am less a person than a series of outfits inhabited across time: perhaps Goya was too, and Hardy and the *Dolly Birds*, each shifting identity shaped by their clothes, even when they're off. Beauty's a role that's also an identity. You can't take it off when you get home and, even if it's not your job, it's a role you're always working: a second shift that may as well be a second career. But models, actresses don't have to commit to their clothes. They leave them at the studio, the shoot. We like them, and we want to be *girls like* them because they are *like* girls. What we like in beauties is not their apparent ease but our knowledge they're working to be *si belle*. For this we forgive them their fame. As for us, we live in our clothes, and every day must put that person on again, however it fits. It is familiar to me to feel slightly uncomfortable: it is comfortable. My clothes shouldn't fit too well, should rub a bit, remind me there's room for improvement, or ways of escape. I could write the story of my life as a catalogue of outfits: everything I've ever done as everything I've ever worn.

Though
It can be exhausting to inhabit new clothes.
It's so difficult to choose the latest thing: something stops me.
I am not *that* person with *that* life
Even if the outfit would help me make it.
Still
There's such a thing as
The beautiful newness of new clothes
Which is *like*
The beautiful newness of the '60s.
Which remains
New, however old
Like bri-nylon.

UNE FEMME MARIÉE—CONCRETE

i

What is the difference between Godard in colour and
Godard in black and white?
What is the difference between his '60s films that star his
lovers, and those that don't?

I can't find the film at first but find the trailer, which
shows the gestures of everyday life—pulling up a sock,
fastening a blouse—as pleasures of conformity: a man and
a woman fitting their young bodies into clothes, feeling a
smug pleasure that the mass-market shells that hold them
in place feel correct, as though made to measure, their
bodies reverse-fetishes that take the place of the objects

of desire that represent them. Like a fetish, everything in *Une femme mariée* foregrounds its opposite (*une femme mariée* is only 'married' when having an affair).

(*une repetition* for the couple in *Weekend*,
which means *rehearsal*:
repetition that comes before not after)
Far from being revolutionary, they want so much to conform.
To an image.

Godard's every image opposes words it replaces, that go unspoken.
Godard's every word overwrites an image.)

'Why won't you let me look at you?' says the man, who complains she is all surface.
He strokes her legs and she strokes them too.
She is seen and he is not.
In other Godards we see the man looking, as well as the woman looking (beautiful).

ii

An empty flat, half moved-into, anterooms not only of place but self: the person in preparation.

(A little electronic device worn round the waist reminds her to stand tall!)

(Though she has forgotten what Auschwitz was.)

She occupies the ambiguous position of ex-secretary (receptacle of secrets), like Bardot in *Le Mépris*.

Her blank-faced acceptance of herself as her own commodity. *(Is this a feminist film?)*

She is desired; she does not desire anyone. Unless it's herself, being desired.

She is refreshingly candid as she never insists on nature.

She sees a model in a magazine who looks like her (it's her?) and, underneath

'What a woman should know' (being a woman is a matter of knowledge?).

She likes to know she is being watched

(by her husband's detective).

She likes to be in the street, moving between private spaces

(in taxis, in shops) the position of the Instagram influencer.

She pauses (the film's most famous shot) in front of a billboard showing a woman many times her size. Perhaps one day it will end, this strange practice of putting women on show: girls bigger than houses—girls small enough to put in your pocket—that began with the twentieth century, that began with film. In the meantime, look at the beautiful woman. I am 'like' her, yet utterly unlike her: the magic of cinema!

(In another part of Instagram, an influencer celebrates the reopening of Paris by going into all the department stores. She is not an artist and this is not a performance: this is her work, or rather what she allows us to see of her work on Instagram. To be on Instagram is to make your life your life's work, and she goes into the department stores not only because she wants to but because she must. I want to go too. It is her living and it is the way she lives her life. Though I influence no one, it is the way I live mine.)

The older guy from the pre-image world tells the young woman that beauty is 'paramount' but he can't explain why. Is beauty a gimmick: a shortcut to—and shorthand for—value? He wants to 'give intellect a break'; her image is his opportunity. A willing object, she wants to 'strip for your husband' as the record tells her, but it plays only the sound of a woman laughing. Who is she laughing at?

(What sort of men does Godard think are in the audience, watching this woman? They have three screen avatars: the husband, the lover, the older man. What sort of women does

Godard think are in the audience looking at the woman? They have only one avatar and that is the woman herself. She is young, beautiful, and thinks about being looked at. Godard cannot imagine other women in the audience. The subject of the difficulty of women's beauty is, for Godard, a subject only for beautiful women. That a woman 'only happens' to be beautiful is so often the case in film: her beauty 'is not part of the story'; we are not allowed to mention it as freakish; we are expected to take it as representative of all women, of ourselves, without investigating what powers ask us to identify with these women without envy, without critique; what powers ask us to abandon the politics of our own lives.)

My dilemma, like Godard's, is:
How to critique femininity and still look cute?

But this time (surprise!), another woman: older, less 'beautiful', still careful with her looks, working as a cleaner (*is* this a feminist film?), says she is 'at one with beauty' during sex. Which means that the rest of the time she acknowledges, despite her neat makeup, that she is not beauty, though she and it occasionally coincide. But her speech (taken from Céline) is an obvious citation: its melodramatic style the opposite of Godard's, its affect more fake here than the fakeness of his modern world.

The characters in *Une femme mariée* don't know they're in a movie. Karina and Belmondo (in *Une femme est une femme*, in *À bout de souffle*) are their own directors, and can make diegetic time stop. *Une femme mariée* is populated by earnest, bad people who want only to inhabit the aesthetic in which they find themselves. They lie earnestly, with only the intent to be dishonest. *Une femme mariée* is not a playful film. Has Godard come to inhabit their earnestness? Despite its good intentions is *Une femme mariée* not such a good movie?

Une femme mariée works better in trailer form, more successful as an advert for itself than an entire film.

BANDE À PART—ANOTHER SHADE OF GREY

Beauty is not how any girl looks, but how she's looked at.
If the camera looks with love, then she is beautiful.
Is beauty discovered or created by it?

Beauty is constant discovery: an eye, a hand, takes on meaning through gesture caught. Godard could only discover Anna Karina once. In *Bande à part* he makes her more awkward; gives her a bad fringe cut in order to rediscover her beauty, moving from long shot to close-up.

In lockdown I am only in close-up. The wrinkles show; why wouldn't they? For work, I read a manuscript by a beautiful woman. I can tell because her heroine does not mention her own body. For beauties, the body is not a constant obstacle.

If beauty is the flipside of violence, it also disguises work, including the work of being beautiful and the violence of that work. In lockdown it is no longer my job to be the most beautiful woman in the world, in a world where being the most beautiful is the job of all women, having, like any job, different ranks and renumeration. The woman industry relies on *one* woman being more beautiful than the rest, who are both more *woman*—as femininity is what has been worked over—but less *woman* for being background to *the* beautiful woman. Because I do not look extraordinary, there is no way for me to look at all. Because my body's only ordinary, I imagine something monstrous. The mirror shows me nothing special: small defects I know I won't outlive. In lockdown I am trying to make myself over, into a woman who is in no way special except for being herself.

(Pinterest: a picture of Anna Karina intoxicated with the luck of her own body. Should I finally accept I am not one of the lucky ones. You choose a look, but you have one body and that is hardly a choice. Why can't I be all the girls at the same time?)

I'm so tired now of women being beautiful in films. Another poster: even the prettiest girls don't look like that untweaked. Can we have avatars that are not beautiful?

Can appearance itself be defemininised? Not *how would that look?* but *how would that feel?*

Is it time for me to accept being 'old'? I see women my age who accepted it years ago: I see others who never will. If I changed my mind, could I go back to the lipstick, the hair dye? Or, once decided, is it for good? And good for what? I hardly have a choice. Beautified I now look not like achievement but attempt. The more the attempt shows, the more it fails. But nor do I feel beautiful when I don't try; I feel ugly. Why do that to myself? Can *ugly* guard me against beauty? Trying to *not* be beautiful is no cessation but an act. I am trying to *do* something with my body—by persistently inhabiting it unbeautified, in public—not only for myself, but for other women.

(The beauty I've demanded of myself is not something I demand of other people.)

Goodbye then, feminine tweaks of the body and mind, many of which I'd already given up on, though not yet formally abandoned. Goodbye (forever?) makeup, long hair, shaving. I feel more myself but don't recognise my picture: *another aul wan.* I don't, however, recognise myself as anything else.

(I buy a new moisturiser online: discounted if I type the word BEAUTY).

Life feels flat without the tension of the temporally impossible: working toward future beauty via Godard's beauties of the past. Instead of looking for another camera to love me, I'd like, just once, to have incarnated beauty, on a photo or film so no one could deny it.

(With no non-relative value: beauty is always on discount, somewhere.)

Sometimes it's hard to believe I haven't lived in black and white.

EARLY SHORTS: CHARLOTTE ET SON JULES, TOUS LES GARÇONS S'APPELLENT PATRICK, UNE HISTOIRE D'EAU, UNE FEMME COQUETTE — PAVING

Day 21 of lockdown: *Charity fun run for your own funeral.*

Today it's not cute to see Patrick put his hands on Charlotte's waist the moment he asks her for a drink, then, when she pulls them off, put them on her shoulder. Does Godard's camera do the same thing?

Before 1960 (*À bout de souffle* was filmed in 1959), Godard's women have short hair. In lockdown my hair gets short, then shorter: first the heroine of *Une femme coquette*, then *Une histoire d'eau, then Charlotte et son Jules*. Or not like them? Not 'feminine'. I can't remember this girl-thing I should resemble. The mirror doesn't tell me and I have no other reflections except for movies full of women who look more like each other than anything like me. Godard continues to insist that sex is *the* difference: *Masculin? Féminin?* There's no third way. If I no longer want to look like Godard's women. I don't want to look like his men either. Losing track of femininity, which never suited me anyway, I seem to have lost track of nothing.

It's not that I don't have a face anymore: I don't look 'like' anything. I have no surface: I no longer 'appear' to be.

> *Without the surface which stands out from the mass of shapes*
> *The line separating things from propositions*
> *The sounds would stick to the shapes and propositions would be impossible*
> *The organisation of language*
> *Cannot be separated from the poetic discovery of surface*
> *It's a question of going back up to the surface and discovering.*
> (Is this from '*un film comme les autres*'?)

If I don't have a face that can appear on films, how can I call it a face at all?

Then I think, like Belmondo in *À bout de souffle:* 'If you

don't like youth; if you don't like femininity; if you don't like beauty... *allez vous faire foutre!*[11] Why continue to desire something I never had? Did I think I had a *right* to become beautiful?

I don't think this lockdown will ever end.

PART II:

COLOUR

LE MÉPRIS—MAGENTA

Bardot: You love me totally?
Piccoli: Yes, I love you totally, tenderly, tragically.
Bardot: Me too.

i

Most people watch films at night, when they're tired. I watch films in the morning, before I get up. Walter Benjamin wrote that a man who tells his dreams before breakfast, 'still half in league with the dream world, betrays it in his words and must incur its revenge.'[12] Will watching a film before breakfast betray, and invite, the revenge of the dream factory?

If cinema is truth at 24 frames per second, truth, in *Le Mépris*, is hidden between the frames of the opening scene in which we *do not* see Bardot raped, assaulted, or insulted by an American film producer with whom her screenwriter husband silently colludes. The unfilmability of this act is the worst thing about it. If Marguerite Duras' films address the melancholy of being a survivor, Godard's films address the melancholy of being a spectator. *Le Mépris* is melancholy because of, not despite, its colour.

The couple is Godard's ethical territory, as Hegel's was the family, and sulk is its methodology. Sulk asks a question while contradicting a statement. Sulk is *j'hésite*: it makes space for an answer which it simultaneously repels. Sulk is one-person dialectic.

Some find Godard's movies romantic, but his love stories are always hate stories: in *Bande à part,* in *À bout de souffle,* couples are mean to each other: *STOP! Le Mépris'* hero is boorish but not charming. Piccoli is not Belmondo (beauty matters for men too). The first time he abandons his wife from cupidity; the second out of cruelty. *Le Mépris* is depressing like *La Chinoise* is depressing, because it's about people who can't value other people: if *La Chinoise* shows the contemptibility of casual terrorism, *Le Mépris* shows the terrorism of casual domestic contempt.

(Godard shoots Bardot, naked, through three colour filters: red, blue, then white, the French flag, the US flag.)

(When Bardot is naked, Piccoli looks overdressed in a shirt and jacket.)

Godard has a thing for half-built roads, for half-built flats. In *Le Mépris,* set on the Côte d'Azur, the windows are too high up the walls in the modern apartment. They are horizontal. This is depressing. Correct windows are vertical and shuttered and run from the floor to the ceiling, almost: Paris windows.

Of course Bardot never escapes to Italy but dies in one of the many car crashes in Godard's movies, prefiguring his own near-death in 1970. As in *Pierrot le fou,* everything ends at the end of France, as far as you can go toward the Mediterranean: les calanques. I've swum there. I jumped from a boat and thought I was going to die, a sea so cold on a hot day it was impossible to draw in breath. But I didn't die. I kept on breathing. I even looked like I might be enjoying myself.

I wished for a negative movie, with no action. On day 55 of lockdown, I bought expensive pink pyjamas, remembering the colour of Bardot's striped blouse as magenta, only to find it wasn't, and that newness both is/is not the answer, and that the narrowness of my own style is not something from which I can easily escape. Fashion that says 'timeless' is inbuilt-outdated. Subtraction to neutral will get you nowhere, as dress is the repetition not of an object, but a feeling. Would you wrap up one of my old dresses and post it back to me, fresh from the store?

WEEKEND—YELLOW

Le Mépris was shot in Technicolor. Godard, working with his director of photography Raoul Coutard, is associated with Eastmancolor, the first commercial alternative to the earlier Technicolor, which used a prism in the camera to expose three strips of film, capturing red, green and blue. Each strip was then independently dyed with the colours' complements (cyan, magenta and yellow), before being transferred to a single print for projection. Doing everything inverse, Eastmancolor produced a 'positive-negative' Monopack film without the need for a special camera; a single negative based on the subtractive colour system, which filtered cyan, magenta and yellow from white light.

Subtractive colour is the mix we're used to—primary colours are mixed to make secondary colours: cyan and yellow make green; magenta and cyan make purple. Mix all three subtractive colours to get black.

Additive colour reverses the mix: secondaries produce primaries: mix all three additive colours to get the ultimate negative: white; green and blue produce cyan; combine green with red and you get not a darker shade but yellow.

(A man's yellow scarf worn by bourgeois Mireille Darc.)

(Yellow shorts worn by bourgeois Juliet Berto when she fights the tractor driver in the *La lutte des classes* sequence.)

(Is yellow a bourgeois colour? Or a comic colour? Both? Why?)

Weekend is about girls who can afford to dress as women. When you look girlish enough you can wear womanly clothes and escape the smear of 'woman'. When a woman wears girlish clothes, this is not the case. She is a joke. There is nothing funny about beauty unless it goes wrong, and a beautiful woman can never be funny because she is beautiful, unless she is funny from the outside, laughed at as incongruous (as beauty does not match everything). I'm obliged to dress like a girl because womanly clothes cost more. I can afford good girl clothes, or poor woman clothes: imitation, synthetic, maldesigned.

(Though even girl clothes are not cheap at all.)

Godard is right: age begins to be unfair. Godard, who stays all the time behind the camera, does not age. By mourning age, I do no more than conform to the aesthetic standards in which he has instructed me. Though he would never pick me, off-screen or on, I am in a Godard movie.

There are so many empty flats in Godard. Someone is always temporary, moving in or out. There are so many ugly modern flats in Godard. His reputation for picturesque Frenchness falls entirely on the beauty of his characters. And Godard really cared about fashion: look how the clothes of Juliet Berto, last seen as a peasant in *La Chinoise*, whose lover is killed by their car's collision with a tractor, are *si bien assorti* with both the vehicles' bodywork: yellow.

(Of Godard's women, only Berto does beauty as comedy against beauty.)

PIERROT LE FOU—CYAN

Karina: You were crazy to do this?
Belmondo: No, I'm in love.
Karina: It's the same thing.

Cahiers du Cinéma: *There is a good deal of blood in Pierrot.*
Godard: *Not blood, red.*[13]

i

Sometimes I spend an hour in aesthetic re-education, trying to see blue in things.

In lockdown I am trying to see the colour of my kitchen. The colours I mean: to find an aesthetic position that can make me see things good. I mean, that can make me see the good in things. I'm trying not to design my life, but to see its design, the underlying tone and rhythm of its colours. I'm trying to take Instagram photos as though what I have were already ideal. I am trying not to make my life into a movie, but to see the movie in my life.

Pierrot le fou is blue: blue skies, blue seas, Ferdinand/Pierrot/Belmondo's blue face. Unlike Technicolor, Eastmancolor film corrupts: cyan fades first: blue skies become white. The colour that lasts longest is magenta.

When Pierrot/Ferdinand describes Marianne as a '*jeune femme en technicolor*', it's translated as 'a woman who looks like a movie star'. I look for the tiny clue of the non-aesthetic. In her, in her surroundings. This is in no way looking for imperfection, which is perfectly part of beauty.

ii

Belmondo's wife wears a girdle. This is why he must leave her.

Karina, if she does, has the indecency not to mention it.

(Perhaps she wears one but preserves the illusion.)

Only at certain angles can I begin to see that Karina and I might be the same species.

I'm fit but my body is deformed—I might say formed—by childbirth. Like Pierrot/Ferdinand's wife, I *could* wear a 'scandale'. Godard does not admire such women. But nor does he admire women who might wear a girdle but refuse. He only admires women who do not have to make that choice. This is no sort of choice. I am aware that in watching Godard's film I am doing myself another obscure violence.

I had waited so long for my moment to become beautiful
I watched out for it carefully but, if it came, I did not see it.
Now I know it has passed me by
But when I look back at old selfies
Maybe I was.
Beauty is never inhabited by the beautiful.

Well.

One of the quickest ways to shut women down is to make them afraid to speak publicly from their imperfect bodies. The trick (*le truc*) is that capitalism had already made bodies a synecdoche for selves. Refuse the mental squeeze of beauty's girdle and my formless self has no boundaries. The temptation to call myself ugly hovers like revolution: it wouldn't take much to accept the challenge. What would be the nature of that revolution: revolution facilitated by the image or a revolution of the image? Or. Also.

Or is ugliness, like beauty, a game no woman can win? There is no zero sum for feeling ugly which is an ugly feeling: shameful, blameworthy. Could I win by refusing to play? Instagram Karina, old, her trademark boater, mascara, and fringe applied to a face that has changed: is this defiance or compliance? I am not the same person as I was even a few years ago, years during which I was trying to make it, years I wore makeup, the time I was younger because I *had* to be. A man in Mexico paid attention not to me but a press-call photo of me photo'd by many photographers: '*You look like a movie star!*' I was transformed in his eyes because the cameras looked at me. He did not turn to me but continued to stare at the photo. My work was no longer my work but a lens through which I could be looked at.

What do I really look like? I have no idea.

The animals in Pierrot and Madeleine's magical land are caged.

In Godard movies

People betray each other.

Karina and Belmondo on their horrible cannibal isle.

In self-isolation.

The sand, the lack of shade.

Wouldn't they rather be in Paris?

Whose paradise is this?

Driving out of Paris (as he drove into it in *À bout de souffle*) lights play across Belmondo's face: red, green, and yellow.[14]

Like green-eyed people, my blue irises, reflecting the camera's glare, turn red.

MADE IN USA—'ORANGE OR YELLOW?'

Again I do not watch *Une femme est une femme*. Perhaps it is not a film to watch alone.

(By now it takes me over a day to watch a Godard movie, sometimes up to three: they have become durational art.)

What Karina does for Godard is *make the difference.*

But in this film there is something monstrous about her difference: her obviously artificial hair and makeup, her Technicolor synthetic knitwear. Eastmancolor film stock was amber, lending a yellow tinge to its colours: its red was tomato, sometimes almost orange, its blue, mediterranean, and its yellow very yellow, sometimes almost orange too. A tiny male detective/gangster arrives. Karina towers over him, a ruler's length. I can't evaluate her anymore. Is she beautiful or does she stand in the gap in the movie where we expect beauty to be? Is she there to be aspired to, or is she just what *is*?

It's no surprise that this is Karina and Godard's last film together. Her face is immobile. Karina was always about turning, hesitating, recognising, then smiling, just a bit, for the camera that stands in for the viewer. More than complicit, it is private. But Karina does not play to the camera here. She is not in collaboration with it, does not control it.

Godard does not insist that she does not do this.

Because her beauty refuses its former function, she has become a mask of her own features, an icon like Dietrich, whose face is shown throughout. Either Godard has hardly anything left for her to do, or she has little left to do with him. She's done it all, from the victims of his first movies, to the bored excitement junkie of *Pierrot le fou*.

Is Anna Karina beautiful at all anymore?

Karina always made the world unreal. If she were to find herself pregnant with a dilemma, like Goya in *Masculin féminin*, she would, as in in *Une femme est une femme*, merely flip the egg. The bigger she gets, the more the plot shrivels. She handles the guns like empty penises; picks them up, looks at them, puts them down again.

There are periods of silence: image and sound separate.

Godard, a god of walls: of flaking paint; of concrete; of peeling posters: primary colours, red, yellow, blue, spends *Made in U.S.A.* looking at Karina against these backgrounds. These walls are exteriors: Godard has never been able to keep Karina inside. It is a visually satisfying film in which the plot reveals itself to be only an enabler of these images.

(In the meantime, Pinterest dials me up another look.)

Karina died in 2019. Remembered in headlines as 'Godard's muse' (in their first short together—directed by Agnes Varda—she played his silent doll-bride), though IRL they set up a joint production company, the trick was he seemed to produce her. In fact, her image would produce his movies, which came to be known as 'Godard movies', the movies in Eastmancolor, movies in which the girl is also the gun.

You can transpose plot and dialogue to any place: Atlantic City to a suburban motel if a girl who stands in the beauty gap speaks the lines, rehearsing the tension of heterosexual narrative. But the love story in *Made in U.S.A.* is already dead. As was Karina and Godard's. Desire offers plot a future, if only temporarily; that's why love works in films, and why Godard's films work best where there's an idealistic, idealised couple, the woman in the traditional role of something to be attained.

What does the woman desire?

On Pinterest Godard himself becomes a subject: I mean, the camera's. Photo'd in black and white, he inhabits a different world to the Eastmancolor women he films. Godard and Karina, she looking out at the camera, which is her job; he looking at her, which is his; Godard is, in fact, unrecognisable without a woman by his side. Sometimes I dress like Godard (blazer, jeans, dark glasses), sometimes like Karina (dolly coat, dolly dress, dolly shoes). Do I want to look like Karina and be treated like Godard (my appearance, a factor of my work), or do I want to look like Godard and be treated (my work only a factor of my appearance) like Karina?

Or do I want to be the double figure:
The image and the filmmaker
Godard and the Godard girl?

UNE FEMME EST UNE FEMME—STONE

I can get tired of staring into anyone's face, even Anna
Karina's. I'd put off watching *Une femme est une femme*
because I'd seen it before, long ago when I was one of
those people who loved *Une femme est une femme*, who
don't love Godard's political movies. It is Godard's first
Eastmancolor film, after which he went back, temporarily,
to cheaper black and white. It is his most beautiful film
because there is no green at all and hardly any yellow, just
the colours of the French flag: red, white and blue.

Red is Anna Karina's cardigan.

Blue is the collar of her sailor suit.

White is the colour of the stone buildings of Paris.
Godard's '60s feature-length Eastmancolor films take

place outside Paris, which is tricoloured black, white and grey. Except this one.

In the red-walled strip club, Karina, wearing white and blue, dances, lit by coloured gels, rendering her skin blue, then red, but it never becomes green, though the shot cuts to the stage lantern so we see the green gel in the rotating colour wheel pass over the light.

Une femmes est une femme is a series of stills made into a moving picture about the practice of being photographed. Its characters are hardly even points of view but appearances: I mean the act of appearing.

Because beauty is a snapshot.

But is revolution?

Or is beauty a matter of *j'hésite*?

Though many of Godard's New Wave films are *about* women, their subject is never quite a subject. Is this because, however outspoken, Karina's motives remain opaque: as the film calls them, 'feminine'? Or is it the way the camera watches her? Always in the third person, seen by the camera like a man who wants her, she turns to it as though knowing she's watched, as though watching herself in performance. We can't identify: only desire.

Desire her, or to be a girl like her.

Angela (Karina) wants to be Cyd Charisse. I want to be Karina performing Angela pretending to be Cyd Charisse. I can hardly see the politics of *Une femme est une femme* because Karina and Belmondo—and their few grim streets around the Moulin Rouge— are now more glamorous than Charisse and Gene Kelly. I want my life to resemble theirs, and to live how and where they live although Paris hardly resembles their Paris anymore.

(By the time he made yet another film about youth, Godard was no longer young.)

When the strippers in *Une femme est une femme* take off their clothes, they reverse-age: no longer girls of the '60s but women of the '50s, wasp-waisted bodies lagging behind their cubic garments. Beauty is built from our obsolescence. The only faces impossible to buy are those on sale in the past. Pay what you like now, you can never get them back.

This item is unavailable.

What calms me is looking at colours.

We still go crazy for the outfits, though, for the girls.

What is a girl? Potential to be something else. In Angela's case, to be—or not to be—a mother. The film was released before my mother was a mother, in one of the last years she had potential to be something other than what she became. How much of that so-called pleasure of youth was feeling the potential and not using it (as use shuts potential down)? How many of the sorrows of age are only the loss of a white screen? To have potential was all that mattered. As for me, I can only appear as aftermath.

(Can men be crazy about girls the way girls are crazy about girls?

Could we have beauty that is not about selling?)

Karina wants a baby.
Or rather, 'Angela'.
I did not.
Karina miscarried—
I did not—
After which she became depressed, briefly institutionalised, then saved, she said, by Godard's offer of a part in *Bande à part*.

(Though she was already married to him, which had played no small part in her depression.)

Does beauty lead to babies, or away from them?
Can having babies be a revolutionary act?
Can beautiful revolution occur in secondary colours?
In *mots vagues*, not *images claires*?

(But, still, how sensible of Karina—like my mother—to have been beautiful when young! My mother's working-class beauty a flag against her fate. How obediently, at the same age—being told it was trivial—I dismissed beauty and any power it might have lent me; becoming, in youth, compliantly plain and powerless.)

Now here I am killing time—as time is killing me—trying to see how beauty can fit revolution, trying to get on with my life even as I'm trying to smash it. After a lifetime of trying, exiting the life in which beauty can play a part, I'm still playing tennis with Godard, lobbing these points back and forth. At what point does a tennis ball become a grenade? At what point is it necessary to explode? And how?

Imagine believing in beauty so much you think it could solve anything.

Or are Godard's films about beauty 'despite', 'yet' and 'anyway'?

Anyway… you get to see Belmondo's real breath in the cold air, really coming out of his body that one time, in that one street in Paris. And Paris is freedom. Again. But, now I am as free to move as anyone else, Paris is no longer there.

Paris, more than anywhere is the movement of its people. They don't have to be from Paris. They just have to believe that Paris is where they are.

Can we take Paris up where we left off?

Are we Paris?

Can there be any cinema at all without beautiful girls?

ALTERNATE ENDING GREEN—THE DREAM LIFE OF GIRLS

i

> Planning to go to Paris I was terrified that
> When I got there I'd have nothing to wear.
> It has taken me a lifetime to dress even this well.

A true story: bored in lockdown I did something I've not done for years: I drew a picture of each item of clothing I own on a sheet of paper, as though seeing myself all at once. Itemising, I found I'm not what I have but what I don't. Used to a quick enough turnover of personality, around the time of my birthday I sold all my clothes. And those I couldn't sell I gave away. I got rid of clothes I liked! Didn't want to get old in them.

ALTERNATE ENDING RED—HOW TO BE BEAUTIFUL FOR THE REVOLUTION

i

I finally got to Paris and everything made me cry.

The women looked different, or I did. I was out of place.

I have missed my chance. I have never been beautiful, and now I don't want to be old.

I'd better change the colour of *I should*.

There is no image for me to be now.

When I got to Paris I cut off my feeds—Pinterest, Instagram—the women on the street were enough. Paris makes money from being itself, having spent its money in order to be itself: fashion is a complete way of life, circular, nose-to-tail, women the interface for

With each, I let something go. What was it? What I could have been?

If we don't buy things, tweets an influencer, *how will we feel?*

I couldn't wear nothing, so I bought some more, mostly other people's clothes. If the moment of feeling alive is the moment of buying, not wearing, then, how to prolong that life or, knowing it's unsustainable, how to create another? Were the clothes I bought more 'age-appropriate'? No, they were girlish. But not a girl from the present, or from any age I have been alive: a girl from a Godard movie.

(Did I think the past was safe?
And safe from what?)

Everyone wants to be in fashion and everyone wants to be timeless. Nevertheless I'm finding it difficult to desire. I don't want *more* anymore, which is—more and more— only more ways to look less like the movies. Still, buying clothes, like making films, is faith in futurity, that there will be somewhere to wear, someone to watch. Now I have them, I don't want to sell myself again. Though no doubt I will.

consumption. Consuming, Paris consumes itself. Or they do. But I could not become them by eating them with my eyes.

(On the boulevard, a man with a mask that said LIFE.)

I passed her on the street. No, she passed me.

Who I'd so often passed in photos of her passing.

Did I notice her? Of course: she was an 'influencer': I knew the colour of her sofa, her walls, her underwear. She was someone with whom I had been intimate, though she had not with me.

Did she notice me? Of course not, not at all.

Stardom is a one-way street.

I'd thought she was one of the more 'approachable' ones but, when I saw, in the flesh of age and class, the gap between us, I knew it's not her I'd been close to, but her image.

The first time I went to Paris I was young and I'd thought there was still time for me to become a Godard girl. But fashion is too fast, and so is art, as well as girls who have the energy and cash to look like this, endlessly replacing each other across time. And oh my god in Paris I couldn't

'*The real hard question,*' says an influencer 'downsizing' her 'closet', '*do I love this or not?*'

What have I done all my life, except made a few images of myself as I might have been in a Godard movie; not even images but attempts at images, failure built-in. But even to try was beautiful… or was it? At any rate I have tried all my life. And I will continue, though the longer I try, the less chance I have of hitting the mark.

Like Godard, I have worked with the difference between images and words.

A working girl, I work with images, because that's what I've been given to work with.

Don't blame me if I work it.

And ask for more besides.

ii

Finally I couldn't go to Paris.
The city shut down and here
I am standing on the edge of autumn, with
The perfect wardrobe
And nothing to do in it.

make art. I only looked at websites of dresses, as though being in Paris were also looking at pictures of Paris.

ii

I finally got to Paris and it was hot.
Too hot. I got
contact dermatitis from a bad soap.
My shoes rubbed
And I was no longer young.
To fear age as a woman is not to fear death
But obsolescence while you're still alive.

But then
I discovered a twist of my hair and suddenly,
everything was right!
I photographed myself and—yes!
(Everything starts with a photograph.
And I look ok in photographs: almost like a woman in a photograph.
Though I don't feel like one. So I take another to make sure.)

How is a woman like an aphorism?
(Narrow, elegant, mysterious.)

There are only so many Godard movies but—as most are filmed not on green screen but the infinite stage of the Paris streets where even Godard could not choreograph the pigeons—each is endless. However enclosed by the Périphérique it's impossible to walk the whole city every visit, and the time spent walking, each time, takes me further away from being a girl on its streets. We exist only to modulate patterns in the landscape and I for one will be sad to leave this life because I will be sad to leave Paris going on without me, with no opportunity to walk down another of its streets, each of them a Godard movie.

All those clothes that meant Paris to me.
And I cannot get there. After all it's required
Not only that we exist for Paris but
Paris exists for us.

Now, having the clothes, it is sad not to have the life to go with them. But fashion acknowledges, as well as the existence of others looking, the fact of knowledge. Fashion—inquisitive—is a way to gain knowledge quickly, and also experience. With the right clothes you can feel in Paris without going to Paris and, however expensive the clothes, that's usually cheaper and more quick.

I've been too bound up with what a woman must be
To imagine what she might become.

iii

Staying in my friend's flat, she had many books about
the art of women of the twentieth century, of the mid-
to-late twentieth century, when Godard and Karina and
Wiazemsky and Seberg and Bardot and Darc and Berto
were making films. And that was a good thing. It was
good that I had this information about these artists: how
else would I know that this art had been made? These
women had made art at a time when it was difficult for any
woman's art to be made, for any woman's art to be seen.
And their art was sometimes, for good reasons, personal:
about their bodies, and their image. Their art was not
always made of their bodies, I mean of photographs of
themselves or filmed performance, but, when it was
not, even when it was abstract paintings, or objects, the
photos in the books hardly ever showed their art without
showing a photo of them too, standing beside. The
camera made the objects beautiful, and the camera made
of the artists beautiful objects. Whatever the intentions of
their art, whatever the content of their lives, they became,
temporarily, screen stars. This is the art of the camera,
the professional camera making its own art. And was this

There are epics waiting to be written on women and clothes! They are the ways we make it through the world, our permitted art. But where is style now there is no street? There's such a thing as not being able to get out of Paris, and it's not unlike not being able to get out of anywhere else. Or like not being able to get out of time.

I have passed some time during my fiftieth year in captivity, watching the films of Jean-Luc Godard. Or rather, watching the women in his films, women fortunate enough to look out at me from the screen.

I will watch them again, in ten years, twenty, if I am still here, as the films will be.

And Godard's women will remain untouched by time as I will not.

Our *point commun*: desire. For a future that can be changed like a change of a dress, a desire to be change, which might start with a green gaze, but there's nothing green about its gaze back. The Godard girl is not an IMAGE CLAIRE. Not extraordinary, never greenscreened, she modulates beauty within her context. She consents to be one note in the music of her city.

I am glad to have been part of this music.

not finally the art that the compilers of the books, even the feminist compilers of these feminist books, wanted and wanted me to see? Art is not innocent of beauty, any more than film.

Maybe I'm not a good enough artist because I don't look good in photos.

Maybe I don't look good in photos because I'm not a good enough artist.

I'm tired of seeing art shown to me as beauty. If beauty is the basis of art, I have no art, not even in the right clothes.

And I started crying in my friend's flat because it began to seem that the women allowed to protest their state through art had, under the green gaze of the camera, come to resemble the state they protested against: white, young, successful and beautiful; straight teeth, toned bodies, modest clothes. The most expensive garment you'll ever own is your own flesh. The trap the camera set them, in order that their art be shown, made it seem that hardly anyone could join them in that protest. Yet the camera's invitation to identify meant I was persuaded that their problem was my problem and that their solutions could be my solutions. But it is impossible to pass through its lens, when that lens also confers distance.

As a white, old, unbeautiful woman, never successful when young, though privileged enough, after many years, to write this book, once I stopped crying I realised that, while valuing their fight, their fight was not quite mine, and it would not help either them or me if I identified too closely. Or this is exactly *why* I stopped crying and it was a huge relief. Goodbye, beautiful girls, and good luck to you in your fight; I don't identify anymore. The camera will never gaze at me with its green eye. Could I proceed without identification, without envy, go direct to my own fight and, though I may have a hard time being heard or seen, be spared some effort that would help neither of us? I don't have to fight beauty because I am not beautiful; I don't have to tear down the walls of social or gender positions I have never occupied. Identification is not helpful here: plain, ordinary and newly old, would you identify with me? Beautiful girls, you have your fight and I have mine. Our fights can help each other's, but I cannot fight through identification with what I am not—what, with time, I am less each day—which would be no more helpful than the aspiration to youth and beauty offered me by what you fight, which shows me necessarily impossible IMAGES CLAIRES in order that I endlessly aspire to them. I am not a Godard girl; I do not live in a Godard movie.

Reverse: *What's revolutionary about beauty?*
To: *What's beautiful about revolution?*

We can't have a revolution for the sake of beauty as it is.

We can't have a revolution without what beauty could be.

Whichever ending you choose,

To be in fashion is to open yourself to discontent.

It is time to switch off the camera. There must be other ways of making art.

ENDNOTES

1   Jerry Gorovoy, 'The Louise Bourgeois I knew', *Guardian*, December 12 2010.

2   Hegel in Anne Carson, *Antigonick*, New Directions, 2015.

3   Many of his later films, made with his partner Anne-Marie Miéville, with whom he has worked since the early 1970s, are unambiguously feminist in intent.

4   'a phrase from a comic strip advertising Internationale Situationniste 11. In French, the phrase is "Il n'est pas de geste si radicale que l'idéologie n'essaie de recupérer".' Sadie Plant, *The Most Radical Gesture*, Routledge, 1992.

5   Jean-Luc Godard, *Le petit soldat*, 1963.

6   'None'

7   'WE MUST CONFRONT VAGUE IDEAS WITH CLEAR IMAGES.' Jean-Luc Godard, *La Chinoise*, 1967.

8   André Breton, *Nadja*, Grove Press, 1928.

9   Most information on 'China Girls' is from Genevieve Yue, *The China Girl on the Margins of Film*, MIT Press, 2015.

10   In 1978 Godard was commissioned by the Mozambican government to make a short film. During this time his experience with Kodak film led him to criticize the film stock as 'inherently racist' since its calibration via 'China Girls' (called Shirley Cards by Kodak) did not reflect the variety, nuance or complexity in darker skin tones. See 'Light and Dark: The Racial Biases That Remain In Photography', *NPR*, 2014.

11   'Go fuck yourself!'

12   Walter Benjamin, *One Way Street: And Other Writings*, Verso, p. 46.

13   *Cahiers du Cinéma*, vol. 171, October 1965.

14   'When you drive in Paris at night, what do you see? Red, green, yellow lights. I wanted to show these elements but without necessarily placing them as they are in reality. Rather as they remain in the memory—splashes of red and green, flashes of yellow passing by. I wanted to recreate a sensation through the elements which constitute it.' Jean-Luc Godard, 'Let's Talk About Pierrot', *Cahiers du Cinéma*, vol. 171, October 1965.

JOANNA WALSH is a multidisciplinary writer for print, digital and performance. The author of eleven books, including *Hotel*, *Vertigo*, *Worlds from the Word's End* and *Break.up*, her most recent work is *Girl Online* (Verso, 2022). She also works as a critic, editor, teacher and arts activist. She is a UK Arts Foundation fellow, and the recipient of the Markievicz Award in the Republic of Ireland. She founded and ran #readwomen (2014-18), described by *The New York Times* as "a rallying cry for equal treatment for women writers" and currently runs @noentry_arts.

Undelivered Lectures is a narrative nonfiction series featuring book-length essays in slim, handsome editions.